Lion

vs.

Tiger

Isabel Thomas

capstone

Heinemann Read and Learn are published by Heinemann,
1710 Roe Crest Drive, North Mankato, Minnesota 56003
www.mycapstone.com

Library of Congress Cataloging-in-Publication data is available on the Library of Congress website.

ISBN 978-1-4846-4073-9 (library binding)
ISBN 978-1-4846-4077-7 (paperback)
ISBN 978-1-4846-4081-4 (ebook)

Edited by Penny McLoughlin
Designed by Steve Mead
Picture research by Svetlana Zhurkin
Production by Katy LaVigne
Originated by Capstone Global Library Limited

Acknowledgements
We would like to thank the following for permission to reproduce photographs: Getty Images: Nature Picture Library/Andy
Parkinson, 19, 22 (bottom right), Nature Picture Library/Anup Shah, 8, 22 (top right, bottom left); Minden Pictures: Elliott Neep,
17; Newscom: Splash News/Solent News, 18, VWPics/Gerard Lacz, 9, 22 (middle left); Shutterstock: apple2499, 20, BBA Pho-
tography, back cover (right), 5, crazycolors, back cover (left), 16, davemhuntphotography, cover (left), e2dan, 14, Eric Isselee, 21,
FCG, 12, Gerrit_de_Vries, 6, Glass and Nature, 13, Graeme Shannon, 10, 22 (top left), Martin Prochazkacz, 7, nale (silhouette),
6, 7, pashabo (texture), cover and throughout, PhotocechCZ, 11, Rostislav Stach, 4, 22 (middle right), Sharon Morris, cover
(right), shin, 15

Every effort has been made to contact copyright holders of material reproduced in this book. Any omissions will be rectified in
subsequent printings if notice is given to the publisher.

Some words are shown in bold, **like this**.
You can find them in the glossary on page 22.

Printed and bound in China
004636

Table of Contents

9-7-19 Penworthy 17.49

Meet the Animals

What has a **shaggy** mane and a loud roar?

It's the **African lion**.

What has striped fur and a long tail?

It's the
Bengal
tiger.

Would a lion or a tiger win in a fight?
Let's find out!

Size and Strength

A lion has powerful shoulder **muscles** for grabbing its prey. A male lion's mane makes him look bigger than he really is.

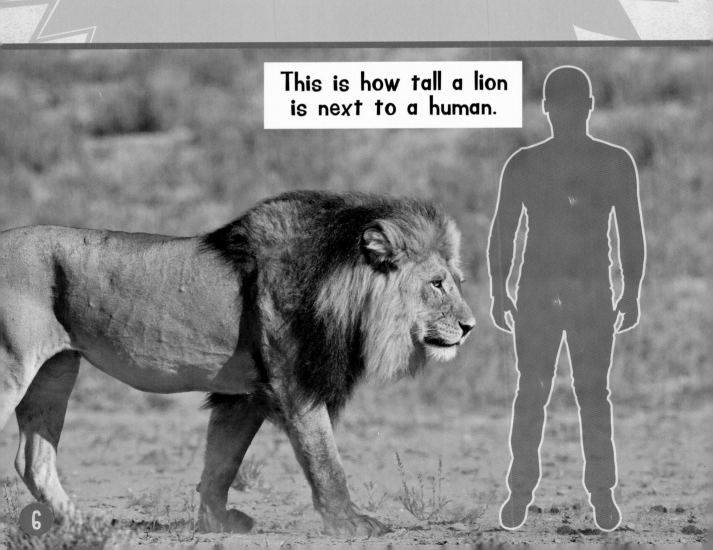

This is how tall a lion is next to a human.

This is how tall a tiger is next to a human.

A tiger weighs as much as 50 house cats! It uses its huge body to knock down animals up to twice its size.

Speed

A lion can only **sprint** for a short time. It will give up if its prey gets ahead. Buffalos are **massive** but slow. They are easier to catch than speedy gazelles.

A tiger is a little faster than a lion. But
it also cannot run for long. Strong leg
muscles make a tiger good at jumping
and climbing.

Coats

A lion needs to hide to get close to its prey before it attacks. Its sandy-colored coat **blends** in perfectly with the pale African grass.

The bright orange coat of a tiger may look easy to spot. But its prey can't see bright colors. The stripes make it harder to see.

Survival Skills

Lions are often called lazy. They rest between meals to save energy. A lion mostly hunts at night, when it's not as hot.

A tiger may have to walk a long way to find food. Tough pads protect its paws from cuts and scratches. It loves to cool off by taking a swim.

Super Senses

A lion has fantastic eyesight. It can spot prey far across the African plains. A lion can see six times better than a human in the dark.

A tiger can twist its ears to hear all around. A tiger's whiskers come in handy at night. They feel tiny air movements that show something is moving nearby.

Deadly Weapons

A lion's bite is 30 times stronger than the bite of a house cat. With its strong jaw and razor-sharp teeth, a lion can kill with a single bite.

paw

claw

A tiger has super-sharp hooked claws that help it catch its prey. When the tiger isn't using them, it hides them in its paws, like a house cat.

Fighting Skills

A male lion will fight to scare off other males or to stop other animals from stealing food. Male lions will often fight to the death.

Lions live in groups, but tigers live alone. A tiger that can't hunt will starve, so it tries to avoid risky fights. Male tigers **wrestle** to scare the weaker one away.

Who Wins?

What would happen if a lion faced off against a tiger? The animals would snarl and roar. They would **wrestle** and try to bite each other.

But who would win?

	Lion	Tiger
Size	8	8
Strength	9	8
Speed	6	7
Energy	7	8
Coats	7	9
Senses	9	9
Claws	7	7
Jaws	10	8
Hunting skills	7	8
Fighting skills	7	8
TOTAL	**80/100**	79/100

LION WINS!

Picture Glossary

blend—fit in well with the things around it

massive—very big

muscle—a part of the body that causes movement

shaggy—thick and untidy

sprint—run fast for a short distance

wrestle—fight by trying to flip the enemy over or hold them down on the ground

Find Out More

Books

Amstutz, Lisa J. *Lions Are Awesome!* (Awesome African Animals!). Mankato, MN: Capstone Press, 2015.

Marsh, Laura. *Tigers* (National Geographic Readers). Washington D.C., 2012.

Ritchey, Kate. *Lion, Tiger, and Bear* (Penguin Young Readers). New York, NY: Penguin, 2015.

Internet sites

Facthound offers a safe, fun way to find Internet sites related to this book. All of the sites on Facthound have been researched by our staff.

Here's all you do:

Visit www.facthound.com

Type in this code: 9781484640739

Index